Wolves

Nancy Gibson

Voyageur Press

Edited by Todd R. Berger
Printed in Hong Kong

96   97   98   99   00   5   4   3   2   1

Library of Congress Cataloging-in-Publication Data
Gibson, Nancy, 1949–
Wolves / by Nancy Gibson
p.   cm. — (World life library)
Includes bibliographical references (p. 71) and index.
ISBN 0-89658-299-X
1. Wolves.   I. Title.   II. Series.
QL737.C22G535   1996
599.74'442—dc20   96-106
CIP

Distributed in Canada by Raincoast Books, 8680 Cambie Street, Vancouver, B.C. V6P 6M9

Published by Voyageur Press, Inc.
123 North Second Street, P.O. Box 338, Stillwater, MN 55082 U.S.A.
612-430-2210, fax 612-430-2211

Please write or call, or stop by, for our free catalog of natural history publications. Our toll-free number to place an order or to obtain a free catalog is 800-888-WOLF (800-888-9653).

Educators, fundraisers, premium and gift buyers, publicists, and marketing managers: Looking for creative products and new sales ideas? Voyageur Press books are available at special discounts when purchased in quantities, and special editions can be created to your specifications. For details contact the marketing department.

Title page: Photo © Alan and Sandy Carey
Page 4: Photo © Gregory M. Nelson
Cover: Photo © Michael Durham/Ellis Nature Photography
Back cover: Photo © Alan and Sandy Carey

Acknowledgments

I would not be writing this book without the guidance of Dr. L. David Mech, who has shared his knowledge, expertise, experience, and enthusiasm for public education about wolves with not only me, but the world.

In addition, I would like to thank Dr. Lynn Rogers, Dr. Ron Nowak, Dr. Djuro Huber, Christoph Promberger, Dave Parsons, Wendy Brown, Jennifer Gilbreath, Dr. Y. Jhala, Dr. Nikita Ovsyanikov, Dr. Tamar Ron, Dr. Steve Fritts, Prof. Iyad Nader, Dr. Naoki Maruyama, Marie-Lazarine Poulle, Dr. Javier Castroviejo, Dr. Dimitry Bibikov, Frank Miller, Dr. Boguslaw Bobek, Dr. Erik Klinghammer, Barbara Kolk, Ilmar Rootsi, and Sergei Pole.

To my Dad—for sharing his wit, curiosity, and encouragement.

Table of Contents

Nature of the Wolf

Suddenly the branches cracked and seemingly out of nowhere two wolves appeared and began to run toward me. I was eye-to-eye with the world's most legendary predator. For me—and my pulsing heart—this was the glimpse of wild wolves that had eluded me for years. I had seen countless tracks and kill sites, heard the chorus of their howls, and even analyzed their scat, but this encounter was worth all of that. Gone were all the tall tales of wolves devouring humans, chasing girls in red capes, and invading the homes of the three pigs, stories that peaked my interest decades ago. These memories were lost as the two wolves approached.

I was in northern Minnesota wolf country with the world's leading authority on wolves, Dr. L. David Mech. When I heard his gasp of excitement as the two wolves plunged from the underbrush, I knew these two merchants of adrenaline were to be a memorable moment for Mech as well, even though he has thirty-five years in the field. We were testing Mech's new "capture collar," a high-tech device that featured two darts with anesthetizing drugs attached to a standard radio-telemetry collar. Mech could send a signal to the computer chips in the collar to trigger the injection of one of the tranquilizer darts, allowing us to capture the wolf for a physical examination. These computer chips also relayed how many times a small drop of mercury bounces in a container, which enabled Mech to monitor activity levels. I was on the cutting edge of research and was witnessing the unveiling of natural-resource mysteries.

Mech pushed the computer button to tranquilize the male wolf. I had assumed we would have to trek farther into the dense, fall-colored woods to find him, but the situation was just the opposite. To our surprise this young loner lurked nearby and had found a new mate! The female wolf ran alongside him shoulder-to-shoulder, cushioning the fall of the drugged male and illustrating the powerful bond of a wolf pack, even a newly formed one. However, once her yellow eyes met ours, her focus changed from helping her mate to escaping the presence of humans and the danger we have represented to this species for centuries.

The drugs took a few minutes to take full effect. Soon we carefully placed the wolf, numbered 215, on bedding and covered his eyes, because darkness lessens the stress of capture. We weighed his sleek body, hoisting

A wolf watches from afar, camouflaging itself with pine branches. Wolves are actually timid and avoid humans. A glimpse of a wild wolf is rare, as their highly developed senses of smell and hearing help them escape our presence. (Photo © Lynn and Donna Rogers)

Yellow eyes are a distinguishing feature of wolves, although brown and even blue eyes have been recorded in adults. (Photo © Bruce Montagne)

his 85 pounds (38 kg) onto a hanging scale, and placed new batteries in his collar. His forty-two teeth were bright, strong, and hardly worn, which indicated he was young, perhaps two years of age. I held his huge feet with their tough pads and thick fur that equip this wolf to travel over many treacherous miles. He is a "dispersal" wolf, meaning he recently left his natal pack to seek a territory of his own with good habitat and especially abundant prey. Wolf 215 survived his initial nomadic trek and lured a mate, and a family of pups could be in his future. As I stayed behind to watch from afar, he slowly awakened from the drugs and grasped his surroundings. The wolf, sensing he was vulnerable, moved to good cover. I felt his mate was nearby, so I ended our intrusion.

Subordinate members of the pack cower when confronted by the alpha wolves. The wolf to the left keeps its body lower than the alphas and licks their faces as a gesture of submission. (Photo © Lynn and Donna Rogers)

In northern Minnesota, large granite rocks web the surrounding pine forests. Huge glaciers left behind these convenient promontories for the largest wild dog, the gray wolf. Fossil history supports the theory that wolves developed in North America from the coyote line. More than a million years ago, a version of the coyote developed a larger skull and massive teeth, and it eventually spread across the continent from Florida to Oregon. The fossils of these animals are almost identical to today's red wolf, *Canis rufus*. The wolf's ancestry then split again approximately 750,000 years ago, developing the ominously titled dirus or "dire" wolf. Dire wolves had powerful legs to roam the plains, consuming mastodons, mammoths, and giant sloths. They weighed around 200 pounds (90 kg) and may have lived in huge packs of sixty to seventy animals. But the dire wolf never left the New World, and it fell to extinction around 10,000 years ago, when weather changes depleted vegetation consumed by its prey. Meanwhile, according to the theory, the red wolflike creatures began intercontinental wanderings when sea levels dropped and Siberia and Alaska temporarily merged. The animal traveled into southern Eurasia and evolved into a similar gray wolf subspecies, *Canis lupus pallipes*, which lives in India, Israel, and Saudi Arabia today. In northern Eurasia about 300,000 years ago, the larger gray wolf developed from some of the wandering red wolves, perhaps in response to cooling climate temperatures. The larger body mass could cope with the cold and prey on larger animals.

Wolves had migrated around the world to become the most widespread land mammal. But human populations also expanded and eventually surpassed their fellow predator. Wolves initially occupied a variety of habitats above 20 degrees latitude, but today they exist in only one half of their former range and in a fraction of their original numbers. Two species remain: the red and gray wolf. The red wolf, *Canis rufus*, has no living subspecies. But the gray wolf, *Canis lupus*, still has taxonomists struggling over the number of wild subspecies. Currently, fourteen are recognized, with five in North America and nine in Eurasia. But there is mounting evidence to add *Canis lupus italicus*, which ranges in Italy. Scientists determine subspecies using ten measurements of the skull, but despite such seemingly exact science for classifying wolves, the debate continues. Nevertheless, the gray wolf, regardless of subspecies, survives in diverse areas. They weigh between 35 and 135 pounds (16–61 kg). Color phases for the "gray" wolf vary from white, brown, reddish brown, or black to streaks of gray, which is the most common.

Exposed teeth and a good stare are often all that is needed to keep order in the social hierarchy of a wolf pack. (Photo © Lynn and Donna Rogers)

Wolves live in packs, which average six members. Scientists use the Greek alphabet to categorize the social hierarchy, beginning with alpha for the top-ranked wolves and ending with omega for the lowest-ranked member of the pack. The alpha male and female are the leaders and are also the root of the enormously powerful bond that cements the wolf pack. The alpha pair are usually the only members to breed, and the two generally lead hunting expeditions, eat first, raise their leg to scent mark (female too), and organize pack activities. As packs have no spare members, the size of a wolf pack is usually dependent on the minimum number of animals that can feed efficiently and raise a family.

The life of a wolf pup begins in mid-spring, approximately sixty-three days after conception. A pup weighs only one pound (0.45 kg) at birth. Litters typically include one to six pups. They rely on a limited sense of smell and hearing during their first two weeks to crawl short distances around their mother and their other siblings. Their first home could be a hole in the ground engineered by the mother and her powerful feet, a cavity beneath a fallen tree, a cave, or even right on top of the ground in a remote region. The den site is within the boundaries of the alpha pair's territory, and the den will be the center of activity for the entire pack over the next eight weeks.

While the pups are beginning to reveal their blue eyes at two weeks of age, their father and other packmates

Two red wolf pups sleeping outside the den. At five weeks of age, these pups have already emerged from the security of the den, met their fellow pack members, and are starting to be weaned. (Photo © Wm. Munoz)

continue to hunt prey and present food to the mother, who temporarily reigns as top dog as the pack furnishes her with food and attention. Introductions of the young pups to their older siblings occur between the third and fourth week when the mother whimpers to urge the pups from the security of their den. The pups are greeted with much fanfare—wagging tails and lots of welcoming licks.

The near-white Arctic wolves live in a barren landscape. They have had fewer negative encounters with humans, which allows close observation by researchers. This pair is consuming a musk ox. (Photo © L. David Mech)

The school of survival starts in earnest once the pups are completely weaned at about six to seven weeks of age. The entire pack now accepts the responsibility for rearing the pups. The pups will frolic and sleep near the den while their packmates hunt for food. If their hunting is successful, the pack will return with some partially digested food in their stomachs, which is regurgitated for the pups to consume. The pups soon learn to lick and mouth the adults' faces, and appear to beg them for food. This is important submissive behavior essential for lower-ranked wolves in order to maintain strong, hierarchical social bonds.

The wolves move the pups to the first rendezvous site at around eight weeks of age. This new site will act as another classroom and is usually near water within the original wolf territory. Sometimes the pups chase rodents and bugs, while the older pack members deliver small animals, carrion, feathers, bones, and other prey parts for the pups to examine and further their knowledge of the sights and sounds of their habitat. Around six months of age, the pups are almost adult height. If there is ample food, the pups will be strong. At this time, they will leave the last rendezvous site and begin to move with the pack across the territory. If food is scarce, then the pups often do not survive.

The territory of a wolf pack is determined primarily by its prey base. When there is a dense population of ungulates (hoofed animals), a wolf pack needs only twenty-five square miles (65 sq. km) to exist. The wider-ranging moose, caribou, and musk ox can expand wolf territories up to 1,000 square miles (2600 sq. km) or more.

Young wolves will often leave the pack when food and breeding competition increases. This is a treacherous time for young dispersing wolves; they need to stay clear of other wolf packs, as well as find a mate and establish their own territory. Radio-collared wolves have traveled 500 miles (805 km) looking for an area with a steady prey base that is void of other wolves. They can maintain these territories for years if the food is abundant.

Wolves are carnivores. They have large canine teeth that bend slightly backwards allowing them to grab their prey. Common prey species include deer, moose, elk, caribou, pronghorn, musk ox, bison, mountain goats, and mountain sheep, some of which can weigh up to ten times more than a wolf. Beavers and hares are seasonal wild supplements. In addition, ranching and the elimination of natural prey has presented domestic livestock as a contentious source of food.

Wolves kill for a living, and their prey base is essential for survival. Given the wolf's cunning ability to determine the vulnerability of prey, teamed with great strength, short bursts of speed up to almost 40 mph (64 kph), and powerful jaws that can crack a three-inch (7.6-cm) femur bone, the wolf represents a formidable predatory force. But a wolf pack will not exert energy or risk injury unless the chances are good for a meal, and even then there is only a slim chance they will succeed in killing their prey. Healthy prey have a defensive system that is equal to the hunting skills of a wolf. Equipped with fleeting speed, they often live in herds, using multiple sets of eyes, noses, and ears to detect wolves and other predators. Much of the wolf's prey base consists of ungulates, whose hooves can be very dangerous to an attacking wolf. I have held a wolf skull with a large hole in the side, the result of a well-placed, fatal kick by a healthy whitetailed deer.

But sometimes the attacking wolves are successful. Visiting a kill site is re-creating nature in the raw. The scattered prey body parts depict the struggles that are commonplace in predator/prey competition. One of the first things researchers do when they find a wolf-killed animal is break a bone to expose the marrow, which reveals the health of the dead animal. All of the dead carcasses I have examined have shown little or no marrow, indicating they were either young, old, weak, or injured animals.

Wolf kills feed their habitats. I have often hiked in Minnesota wolf country and knew I was near a kill site by hearing the noisy ravens perched in trees, anxious for their turn eating a carcass. Wolves clean the carcass, but the remnants are an important food source for the scavengers like eagles, vultures, weasels, rodents, song birds, and insects. The decomposing body also nourishes the soil.

Wolves can devour huge amounts of meat, sometimes up to twenty pounds (9 kg) per wolf at a time! After they gorge themselves, wolves tend to rest for a few days with several visits back to the carcass, especially if it is a large animal like a moose. It is feast or famine for wolves, as they may not eat for another week or more after a successful hunt. On average, wolves need two and a half pounds of meat (1.1 kg) daily to exist, but to reproduce

A wolf keeps an eye on other pack members while it eats. Alpha wolves typically eat first, but other members get impatient and try to grab food before their turn. (Photo © Lynn and Donna Rogers)

successfully they require about five pounds (2.2 kg) daily. That adds up to an annual equivalent of about eighteen adult-sized deer per wolf.

The body language of wolves is intense and clearly demonstrated around a kill site. Wolf communication includes facial expressions, as well as the positioning of the tail, shoulders, and ears. The alpha pair is first to eat from the carcass, while subordinate members wait impatiently. As they feed, the alpha male and female hold their tails straight out, keep their ears forward, and appear more confident and aggressive than the rest of the pack. They will often growl and nip at their packmates if they get out of order. The lower-ranking wolves will often approach their leaders with their tail tucked under their legs and their ears pressed against their head while licking their parents' mouth, literally begging for an opportunity to eat. An intense stare and a good show of teeth are often all that is needed to maintain the complicated social relationship of the pack, but some encounters require younger wolves to lie on the ground exposing vulnerable body parts, a way of asking for an apology.

Powerful legs help excavate dens of all sizes. This wolf is digging into the cool ground to escape the bugs and heat of summer. (Photo © Alan and Sandy Carey)

I once watched two wolf yearlings hunt hare in the High Arctic, and it was interesting to watch the power shift when the alpha pair was over a hill. The young female, which we named Explorer, won the competition of catching hares. After her second catch, she aggressively stood over the hare with her tail erect and teeth glaring at her sibling. She was tired from the hunt, and her sibling tried to take advantage of her fatigue, but Explorer had learned well from her parents to stand her ground. Her sibling looked irresistible as he wiggled and rolled his way near the carcass, pretending not to look at the tempting food. Though the male wolf was not to get the prize from his wary sister right now, Explorer later showed her inexperience by digging a hole and caching the food under the watchful eye of her brother, who then took advantage of the unattended food and his sibling's naiveté.

Despite popular myth, a full moon is not required for wolves to use another important form of communi-

It is a common myth that wolves only howl during a full moon; in reality, they will howl any time of day. However, howling is usually detected during the evening hours when human congestion has quieted down. (Photo © Lynn and Donna Rogers)

cation—howling. I have heard them howl any time of the day and night. Howling, in fact, plays many roles. It excites the pack, motivating them toward some form of action. It is also a "no trespassing" signal to other wolves. Wolf packs must keep competing wolves out to maintain their prey supply. In addition, howling gathers the pack for a hunt, and it is used to reunite pack members after a hunt or other activities. The alpha pair usually starts the

drawn-out wail, and other tail-wagging members quickly respond, sometimes pressing against each other, symbolizing their team. Wolves howl in different chords enabling them to sound like a larger pack. Pups whine at a young age until their vocal chords mature. The howling of wolves is one of nature's primeval sounds.

A ten-week-old female pup eagerly howls with her pack. The young wolf's pitch is still high, but in a few months her howl will be deeper and hard to distinguish from the adults. (Photo © Lynn and Donna Rogers)

Howling can be heard over great distances, from one to ten miles (1.6–16 km) depending on wind and other conditions. Researchers often use howling to locate wolves and track their behavior. In my first summer in the High Arctic, Mech and I waited for a rare calm day to test the hearing and howling response of Arctic wolves. We moved five miles (8 km) away from the research pack, but we could still observe them through our binoculars. Mech cupped his hands around the edge of his mouth and emitted a deep howl. We moved toward the pack and repeated the process. No response. We moved to four and one half miles (7.2 kilometers) away and had just started to inflate our lungs with air when Mech told me to turn around. Another pack of three wolves stood there staring at us with wonderment! After a short while, the wolves stealthily began to circle us with curiosity, probably investigating these two-legged howlers. We later feared that the two wolf packs would fight, since our presence interrupted wolf territorial guidelines. We crawled and gently howled, trying to communicate that we were not intruding. The wolves sat on a hillside and watched our tactics till boredom struck, and they then wandered off without a fight.

While howling is the most notable wolf sound, the complicated communication system of a pack also relies

A wolf is always alert for signs of danger, a change in pack member behavior, or the possibility of a meal. (Photo © Lynn and Donna Rogers)

on growls, whines, whimpers, and barking to signify an alarm. All of these behaviors are easily evident to humans. But it is the sense of smell, which some claim to be one hundred times more efficient than a human's, that is critical in defending territory. Wolves scent-mark the outer edges of their territory by frequently urinating on trees, rocks, and shrubs. To express ownership, the alpha male, female, and sometimes a high-ranking male will raise their legs and squirt strong-smelling urine. The other members of the pack urinate by squatting. Scent-marking and howling are the most energy-efficient warning systems for wolves. But while howling immediately reveals the current location of a pack, scent-marking warns for several weeks. Surrounding wolf packs usually stay clear of scent-marked boundaries to avoid conflict, but if the scent-marks smell old, neighboring wolves may attempt to invade the new territory and expand their present range.

Territorial disputes between wolves will often end in death, which is the leading cause of mortality in areas of high wolf density. Human persecution, starvation, disease, and natural accidents, such as drowning, affect other wolves. In the wild, wolves rarely reach ten years of age, although in captivity, such life spans are quite common.

Overall, the statistics did not favor wolf 215, the wolf we examined in northern Minnesota. In fact, that wolf died the following winter, a victim of other wolves in a hard-fought territorial battle. We do not know the fate of his mate.

Wolves living in cold climates grow a thick inner fur lining that is efficient at blocking out the bitter temperatures. Wolves often curl up and place their bushy tail over their nose and face when sleeping in cold weather. (Photo © Lynn and Donna Rogers)

Decades of research have dispelled some of the fantasies that have enshrined the wolf's existence. Yes, it is safe to walk in wolf range; there has never been an attack by a healthy wild wolf on a person in North America. The wolf is actually rather shy, and scientists are working hard to provide a realistic portrait of this intriguing animal. The wolves are working hard as well. Despite the premature death of wolf 215, he provided valuable information on a species surviving a rugged existence—not fairy tales.

Lupine Lore

The wolf has strongly influenced humanity. It has been a phantom of dreams, obscure images, and myths that have little to do with the true nature of a wolf. The symbolic wolf stimulates some of humankind's most frightening passions towards wildlife. We have been weaned on wolf tales depicting the wolf as a hostile sinner, clever animal, powerful beast, and in Russian stories as the "gray fool." Hollywood enhanced these dramatic characterizations and produced further misrepresentations of the wolf. Many people seem to be content with the old folktales and the celluloid versions of the wolf.

Early cultures feared and yet revered the wolf, primarily due to the wolf's passionate hunting techniques and probably also because of early society's close, day-to-day living with the complexities of nature. Prey was plentiful, so humans and wolves coexisted peacefully. Wolves appear on some ancient pictographs, headdresses, and medicine bundles. Etruscan and Roman legend tells of Romulus, the mythical founder of Rome, and his twin brother, Remus, being suckled by a wolf, and Rudyard Kipling's *The Jungle Book* depicts wolves as rescuers. But in Dante's *Inferno* (1481) in *The Divine Comedy* the wolf is associated with greed and fraud, and the habits of seducers, hypocrites, and liars are called the "sins of the wolf."

While some wolves were successfully domesticated into various forms of a pet dog, their wild counterparts supposedly embodied all forms of evil. A twelfth-century natural-history book asks, "For what can we mean by the wolf except the Devil?"

Even in the modern age, the belief that wolves are evil still exists, but in the Middle Ages, this type of thinking led not only to the killing of real wolves, but also to vicious cruelty against other humans. The idea of the werewolf, a strange mixture of human and wolf, can be traced back to Greek mythology, when Zeus turned his rival, Lycaon, King of Arcadia, into a wolf. In Medieval Europe, the belief that people could turn into wolves led to horrifying attacks. The werewolf trials of this period are flagrant examples of historical attitudes towards wolves that led to the killing of innocent and probably mentally ill people simply because

A wolf will stay close to a large kill, such as this moose, for several days until it is completely consumed. A single wolf can kill an animal ten times its weight, which is a frightening thought for some humans. (Photo © D. Robert Franz)

they roamed at night. In September 1573, a court in eastern France authorized peasants of all villages in the region to "assemble with pikes, halberts [ax-like weapons], arquebuses [primitive guns], and sticks, to chase and to pursue . . . to tie and to kill without incurring any pains or penalties" any and all werewolves infesting the area. The peasants found Giles Garnier, a local hermit, and dragged him to the place of public execution,

This Etruscan statue depicts the lactating she-wolf of one of the most famous legends regarding wolves: that a wolf nursed Romulus, the mythical founder of Rome, and his twin Remus.

where he was burned at the stake. The justices and the peasants were particularly upset because Garnier allegedly "performed his cannibalistic deeds" on meatless Fridays. Many others were victims of such frenzies.

In addition to mentally ill people and antisocial individuals, some of the "werewolves" may have been targeted for wholly medical reasons. Today, scientists have identified a rare disease that is responsible for excessive hair growth on the face and upper body. The disease, known as congenital generalized hypertrichosis, is cited as a plausible source of werewolf stories.

Wolf tales circle the globe. Estonian and Latvian folklore, as well as clerical writings from the same region, claim that non-rabid wolves ate 111 people—primarily children—between 1804 and 1853. In 1809 alone, the literature states, 45 victims died. Many children were killed that summer by "old, lonely, and crippled wolves sometimes alpha females needing food for their cubs whereas rabid wolves only killed in the winter." The Japanese have a story of a young boy who saves a choking wolf by retrieving a bone from its mouth. The appreciative wolf later returns with a pheasant for his friend, but the boy's peer becomes frightened at the sight of a live wolf, and the wolf's offering is refused. Russians say that "wolves are fed by their feet," referring to their ability to hunt large territories and the dexterity of their large feet, which readily spread out like a snowshoe or pull together to reduce friction with the ground. In Germany, there is

The stereotypical evil, beastlike features of the wolf are highlighted in this early drawing.

the story of a fox outsmarting a wolf after luring the wolf into a beekeeper's cellar. The fox ate only a small share of the honey, but the wolf feasted and then could not get back through the window to escape. A slightly more dramatic story comes from Scandinavia. Fenrir was an enormous wolf and son of the god, Loki. Other gods decided Fenrir was becoming troublesome, so they bound him in a special natural webbing called Gleipner. As he howled in protest, a sword was thrust down his mouth, and the blood from the wound formed the River Von. Fenrir finally broke free from the Greipner only to fight the gods in a climactic battle that left the wolf dead and the world consumed by fires and boiling waters. In time, a new sun appeared, and grasses and flowers bloomed to begin a new earth.

A wolf exposing its strong canine teeth is a threat to pack mates, especially during feeding. Large teeth also enhanced the myths about evil wolves. (Photo © Lynn and Donna Rogers)

Certainly people are not fond of being prey, but the thought of such an event feeds a good story. Even as recent as 1911, international newspapers reported outlandish accounts of wolves devouring a wedding party of 118 people. The stories claimed that the children and women were sacrificed first, but the wolves then ate the men and were not satiated until they had consumed the bride and groom. In addition, popular fairy tales of today stretch the imagination of children into believing stereotypical views of wolves. For example, in "Little Red Riding Hood," the wolf impersonates a grandmother in hopes of swallowing a little girl. In the "Three Little Pigs," wolves are tenacious in their pursuit of hogs in their homes.

The movie industry has perpetuated wolf myths by depicting horrific scenes of wolves attacking people in *White Fang*, and showing death and destruction caused by mysterious bites in the recent *Wolf* production. Some movies do reflect the evolving positive attitudes toward wolves, such as *Dances With*

A wolf uses the body of a packmate as a head rest. Wolves demonstrate family cohesiveness by staying in close contact. (Photo © Lynn and Donna Rogers)

Wolves and *Never Cry Wolf*. But even these portrayals stretch the true natural history of wolves by including a lone wolf befriending a man and wolves subsisting on mice.

Without a doubt, the wolf has played a key role in frightening the human psyche and stirring up our collective imagination. But why the wolf? Many theories exist, but most conclude that the wolf is feared because it is a nocturnal animal, and because it is often heard but, due to the wolf's timid nature, rarely seen. These facts give a certain mysterious aura to the wolf. This, combined with the wolf's predatory instincts, sustains the belief that wolves are dangerous to people. Humans want to control what is perceived as a threat, especially if that threat competes for food. People and wolves share the top of the food chain. In addition, it is easier to believe in old tales passed down through generations than to accept new information that has made the wolf so much more intriguing.

Even in an era of detailed scientific study of the true nature of wolves, many of the stereotypical views survive. Politicians use wolf legends when comparing welfare recipients to wolves that are "reluctant to re-enter the wild." The term "a wolf in sheep's clothing" has described many a legislator, and how many times has the proverb "to be thrown to the wolves" been used? The fairy tale song "Who's Afraid of the Big Bad Wolf?" has been altered for every cause imaginable. Hungry eaters "wolf" down their food, and a sexual whistle is called a "wolf whistle." However, the world heard a positive and tearful description in 1995, when Noa Ben-Artzi publicly eulogized her slain grandfather, Israeli Prime Minister Yitzhak Rabin, by saying "you are our hero, lone wolf."

Worldwide, scientists are eagerly studying wolves and educating people in order to slay wolf myths and stereotypes. Some of their work is attracting strong support. But wolf advocates too often paint the wolf as a victim and have used the plight of the wolf to successfully close roads in natural areas and limit timber harvests. Ironically, wolves often travel along lumber roads and prey on deer, which prefer the new plant growth sprouting where the trees had been. Accepting the role of the true wolf is also accepting the role of wilderness. There is nothing like the mournful howl of a wolf to remind us of our complex existence.

Black wolves often seem even more mysterious than their gray counterparts. (Photo © Lynn and Donna Rogers)

Wolves move tirelessly with a fluid motion. They usually travel at a trotting pace, unless they are near prey or danger. (Photo © Lynn M. Stone)

Wolves of the World

The two species of wolves—red and gray—and the fourteen recognized subspecies of the gray wolf have similar natural history and behavior, except in size and adaptations to their individual habitats. They are commonly named for the area and habitat where they occur. Human persecution has forced wolves into remote corners of the world, and in some cases, humans have influenced their social behavior, breeding habits, and mates. The following information includes the known facts about several of the subspecies, but in many cases there is little accumulated knowledge about the animal, or even worse, little concern.

Red Wolf (*Canis rufus*)

The red wolf is aptly named for its reddish brown pelage, which helps distinguish it from the larger gray wolf. The red wolf's fate seemed doomed in 1980 when it was declared extinct in the wild. The southeastern United States was officially void of one of its top predators. But a decade earlier, scientists had scanned eastern Texas and western Louisiana for remnant red wolves, and after numerous attempts, they captured fourteen of the animals. Researchers began to work overtime to save a species that soon was to exist only in captivity. Thus began the new and complex science of restoring a carnivore to its former habitat while enhancing its possibilities for long-term survival. Red wolves had to be taught to hunt by their captors, but at the same time, they had to learn to be wary of humans. The captive wolves, called "founders," successfully reproduced, allowing forty-two wolves to be set free on southeastern coastal islands and two mainland sites by the end of the experimental phase of the project in 1993. Monitoring and research are a continuing component of the program.

The reintroduced wolves have bred, and third generation wolves are currently expanding into native forests, marshes, and agricultural fields in Alligator River National Wildlife Refuge in eastern North Carolina, Tennessee, and in Great Smoky Mountains National Park on the border between the two states. The high population of deer in the region gives the wolves immediate access to food, which enhances their viability. The project is a biological victory, with an estimated fifty-five to seventy-five red wolves ranging free in 1996.

The red wolf's ancestors once lived as far north as Illinois and as far west as Texas. Human conflicts caused the population to dwindle to very small numbers, and it is still disputed whether they interbred with coyotes in order to survive, thus creating a hybrid rather than a true red wolf. After several DNA comparisons in 1991, the U.S. Fish and Wildlife Service concluded that the red wolf is not a hybrid, but some still question the results. Little

Top: A red wolf peers through tall grass. (Photo © Tom and Pat Leeson)
Bottom: A red wolf has larger ears, similar to other wolf subspecies living in warm climates. Big ears help cool the animal. (Photo © Alan and Sandy Carey)

was known about this species until the recovery project raised, radio-collared, and released the wolves.

Red wolves weigh between 50–70 pounds (23–32 kg), and stand 20–32 inches (51–81 cm) tall at the shoulder. They are primarily nocturnal. The basic social unit is the mated pair, which breeds once a year and produces an average of five pups. The pups remain with their parents until around eighteen months of age when they become self sufficient. They then travel up to twenty miles (32 km) away to form a new territory.

Red wolves live in approximately twenty square miles (52 sq. km) of habitat that is also home to several prey species, such as whitetailed deer, raccoons, and nutria. As red wolf populations grow and disperse, private landowners will become an integral component in their survival. The red wolves will need important corridors of good habitat to keep their genes as diverse as possible. The success of this may rely on the tolerant behavior of humans more than wolf habits.

Gray Wolves
Mexican Wolf (*Canis lupus baileyi*)

The southernmost and smallest subspecies of the gray wolf in North America is also the most endangered. The Mexican wolf, often called by its Spanish name "lobo," is generally thought to be extinct in the wild, although unverified sightings have been reported recently in the remote region of the Sierra Madre Occidental in northern Mexico. Lobo once flourished in the mountainous regions of the southwestern United States and central Mexico. These wolves preferred the oak and pine forests usually above 4,000 feet (1,220 m) known as "sky islands," not the desert as many may presume. This habitat is also home to mule deer, whitetailed deer, javelina, jackrabbits, elk, and pronghorn, all prey species for wolves.

The natural behavior of the wild Mexican wolf is only guesswork since humans destroyed the intact wild populations before they could be studied. Livestock ranches and the exploitation of natural prey led the wolves to conflict with humans over food. In 1916, a federal agency called Predatory Animal Rodent Control was formed primarily to exterminate the Mexican wolf. By 1925, the Mexican wolf population was seriously depleted and scattered. The last wild Mexican wolf in the U.S. was killed in 1970.

Scientists think wild Mexican wolves may have behaved slightly differently than northern subspecies, because the hotter and drier habitat results in scarcer prey. Most of the recorded biological observations are from the very trappers and hunters that persecuted the wolves. Even the scientific name of the Mexican wolf honors the government's lead exterminator, Vernon Bailey.

In 1977, with help from the Endangered Species Act, the government hired an old type of trapper for a new type of mission—live capture. Roy McBride was sent to Mexico's northern states of Durango and Chihuahua to live-trap Mexican wolves in order to found a captive population that would produce wolves for later reintroductions. In three years, McBride captured only five wolves. Those wolves are the roots of the current 139 wolves held in captivity in twenty-one facilities in the U.S. and five in Mexico. A Mexican wolf recovery plan is underway to examine reintroduction, recolonization, and recovery areas that could become the home for at least 100 in their historic mid- to high-range elevations. The reintroduced population will have an "experimental, non-essential" designation similar to the status of other reintroduced wolves. This allows for greater flexibility in research and in management of the wolf population.

The Mexican wolf has a long, distinctive mane around the neck, which highlights the richly-colored coat, a blend of gray, brown, black, and rust on top with buff colors underneath. In addition, the tail, ears, and legs often have black highlights. The Mexican wolf is about 10 percent smaller than its northern cousins, weighing 50–90 pounds (23–41 kg) and standing 28–32 inches (71–81 cm) at the shoulder. Captive wolves give birth to four to six pups in April or May, after sixty-three days of gestation.

The recovery of Mexican wolves faces many challenges. There are complex requirements to maintain genetic diversity from such few founders and to preserve the characteristics required for survival in the wild. The final threat however will be a battle with the Mexican wolf's top competitor—humans. Two areas are under consideration for the Mexican wolf's initial return to the southwestern U.S. Success will require further human intervention and, most importantly, education, to insure the howl of the Mexican wolf is heard again.

Plains Wolf (*Canis lupus nubilus*)

Most of the information known about wolves has been collected since the 1930s in the state of Minnesota, the principal, present-day home of the plains wolf. Five hundred wolves have been radio-collared and tracked since the early 1960s in the northeastern part of the state, which is only a minuscule portion of this subspecies' enormous range. This wolf is missing from much of its original range in the United States, but it still has a stable population in Canada. The plains wolf was able to narrowly escape the U.S. government's quest for extinction by retreating to remote areas. In addition, an ample supply of neighboring wolves in Ontario quickly filled any voids created by the government campaigns. The 1960s hold the distinction of having the lowest number of wolves in the continental United States since European settlers arrived; all 400 to 600 wolves of that era lived in Minnesota.

Top: A Mexican wolf awaits its freedom. These wolves are thought to only exist in captivity. (Photo © Tom and Pat Leeson)
Bottom: A thick mane distinguishes the Mexican wolf from other subspecies. (Photo © Wm. Munoz)

Top: Wolves are well known for their excellent sense of smell, which is thought to be eighty times better than a human's. (Photo © Lynn and Donna Rogers)
Bottom: Wolves circle each other howling, which stimulates the pack to hunt. (Photo © Lynn and Donna Rogers)

In 1973, the Endangered Species Act gave the surviving wolves full protection; and in 1978, the population increased enough in Minnesota to change the listing from endangered to threatened.

The plains wolf population has grown steadily at about 5 percent a year since the late 1970s, and today Minnesota hosts over 2,200 wolves. They have in fact saturated the northern half of the state and are moving into some unsuitable agricultural areas and increasingly preying on more livestock. Wolves live in a region with 350,000 cattle, 38,000 sheep, and thousands of other livestock. In 1995, seventy-eight wolves were killed by U.S. Department of Agriculture Animal Damage Control officials for killing livestock. It was verified that the wolves killed 147 domestic animals. In addition to the destruction of the offending wolf, the farmer is compensated. Overall, such losses affect less than one percent of the animals living in wolf range. The program has been hailed as a good compromise and used as a model for other states. But the Minnesota plains wolf population has been critical to the recovery of wolves in the Midwest. Wolves have moved east, crossing major highways into Wisconsin and the Upper Peninsula of Michigan, where each state now hosts 70 to 80 animals. North and South Dakota officials have spotted lone wolves for several years, and it is now thought that several packs have formed. They also range widely. One wolf was tracked to Saskatchewan, 550 miles (886 km) from its home in Minnesota, proving wolves will travel long distances to settle new territories. Wolves can disperse from their natal pack any time of year, but dispersal tends to happen more frequently in the winter, followed by the month of April.

Research on this wolf and other Minnesota plains wolves has made a large impact on our understanding of this complex predator. (Photo © Lynn and Donna Rogers)

In Minnesota, whitetailed deer comprise 80 percent of wolf prey, but farther north plains wolves pursue caribou and moose, while in their western range, they favor elk and bison. Wolf packs require 30 to 150 square miles (78–390 sq. km) of territory hosting about 200 deer for every wolf. The wolves live in relatively low densities amounting to about one wolf per 15 square miles (39 sq. km) or one pack per 60 square miles (156 sq. km).

As with most wolves, this subspecies requires habitat that has a low density of humans as well as adequate cover and food for themselves and their prey. The vast clear-cutting of forests have actually enhanced whitetailed deer populations, which prefer to browse on newly sprouted trees. In addition, the logging roads provide easier access for the wolves to roam their territory. Wolf tracks, scat, and scent-marks are common sights along roads in northern pine forests, but it is equally at home on the prairie and in the deciduous forests.

The adult female weighs approximately 65–85 pounds (29–38 kg), while the male is slightly larger, weighing 80–110 pounds (36–50 kg). The pack size averages six wolves, although packs of fifteen have been found. More than two hundred scientific papers on the Minnesota plains wolf have been published since 1960, creating a centerpiece for global research and education. This accumulated research is the best tool to ensure future wolf survival.

Conserving energy and sleeping, sometimes up to twenty hours at a stretch, is an important survival strategy for Arctic wolves. (Photo © L. David Mech)

Arctic Wolf (*Canis lupus arctos*)

The home of the Arctic wolf is what many have described as a hybrid moonscape, located hundreds of miles north of the nearest tree. The Arctic wolf is easily recognized as the only subspecies with a thick, near-white coat, which provides camouflage in the snow and warmth in the frigid temperatures of the High Arctic. Arctic wolves eke out a living on the large islands in the Arctic Ocean, approximately north of 70 degrees latitude. Perhaps not surprisingly, almost all of what is known about the Arctic wolf comes from summer observations. Their winter activities, much of which is in total darkness, may never be known.

Their ears are somewhat smaller and rounder than other subspecies, and the muzzle is slightly shorter. These adaptations—along with slightly shorter legs—decrease the exposure of their extremities to the cold. Arctic wolves often weigh over 100 pounds (45 kg); heavier weights concentrate body mass for warmth. The wolves have to endure temperatures often dipping to -70°F (-57°C) and constant winds. The cold weather conditions have prevented humans from "taming" their territory and persecuting the wolves. Unlike many of its fellow subspecies, the Arctic wolf is not endangered.

Arctic wolves are easily seen in this treeless landscape, and sometimes close encounters are possible. These factors have made it a fertile research area. The close observations of these Arctic wolves have uncovered many wolf secrets that also apply to the other subspecies. Arctic wolves live with smaller prey populations, so their territory has to be large—more than 1,000 square miles (2600 sq. km) in many situations. Accordingly, the density

An Arctic wolf pup nuzzles its mother for attention, while its litter mate is curious about the activity below. (Photo © L. David Mech)

of Arctic wolf populations is low in this landmass of 2.3 million square miles (6 million sq. km). In the Queen Elizabeth Islands, above 74 degrees latitude, there are approximately 200 wolves, whereas in the southern tier of the High Arctic, including parts of Baffin Island, there are estimates of 3,200 wolves. The High Arctic desert terrain receives some snow seasonally and grows enough fresh grass to support a few prey species, such as caribou and small herds of the prehistoric musk ox, as well as Arctic hare, lemmings, and some birds.

Social bonding and intense training for survival are quite evident. Litters include one to six pups, and they are born slightly later than their southern counterparts, usually around the end of May. Once the pups emerge from the den at three weeks of age, the social interactions among members of the entire pack focus on the pups. The yearlings are often playmates and babysitters while the other pack members hunt. The pups romp with the yearlings near the den, adding intensity to the play behavior that will strengthen the pups and test their body skills needed later for survival. The adults bring back food, and the more aggressive pups get the better share of the catch. Body parts of prey are a common sight around the den, and the parts are true-to-life toys for the pups. Every movement fine tunes their survival skills, whether it be sleeping (sometimes up to nine hours at a time), playing, yawning, or howling.

Researchers in the Arctic have observed adults with their yearling children after failing to reproduce new offspring. These yearlings still receive preferential treatment from the adults. In one personal observation, the adults bellowed a howl signaling the yearlings to follow. The youngsters returned the howl but refused to leave, like stubborn teenagers. After several howls, the adults returned to their offspring, with much jubilation on the part of the one-year-olds—especially toward the alpha male. The intense, submissive behavior was indicative that he was still providing food. In fact, we later observed the alpha male relinquish his freshly-caught hare to a yearling and help ambush another hare for the second young wolf.

Unlike their southerly relatives, which have suffered greatly from the effects of "civilization," it is thought that Arctic wolves still roam 95 percent of their former range, with only limited threats from fur trappers (for their coat valued at $600), oil drilling, and adventurous humans anxious to experience the Arctic.

Eurasian Tundra Wolf (*Canis lupus albus*)

A famous Russian hunter wrote a century ago that the wolves in Russia are "timed to periods of destitution and social disorder among humans." The fluctuation of wolf populations and human chaos is clearly linked in the former Soviet Union even in the remote, northern climate that the Eurasian tundra wolf, sometimes referred to as the Russian tundra wolf, calls home. Wolf populations are currently increasing, taking advantage of the social and economic changes. Fuel for helicopters is too expensive, greatly reducing the number of hunters that can take to the skies, and poison production has been halted. This is good news for wolves, especially these northern wolves, which are vulnerable to aerial hunters in their open tundra landscape. In earlier years, the pressure from helicop-ter hunters drove some of the wolves into the taiga forested region, where they interbred with a southern subspecies, *Canis lupus lupus.*

The Eurasian tundra wolf lives along the fringes of land adjacent to the Arctic Ocean above 65 degrees latitude. Unlike the Arctic wolf (*Canis lupus arctos*), these wolves are not all white or cream colored; most wear more of the traditional gray color combinations with shades of silver blue. The tundra wolf is large, with adults weighing 75–145 pounds (34–65 kg) and standing 28–38 inches (71–97 cm) tall.

These wolves have been eliminated from some of the Arctic islands, such as Wrangel Is-land north of Siberia. But, due to a scarce prey base that is typical of the northern climates, they

Eurasian tundra wolves are expanding their territories because their human persecutors are facing economic problems that prevent them from buying ammunition and fuel for aerial hunting. (Photo © Nikita Ovsyanikov)

do roam widely in small numbers throughout much of the wide-open Eurasian Arctic. Researchers say there are approximately one to ten wolves per 620 square miles (1,600 sq. km). It is believed that Russia has two-thirds of the reindeer (caribou) population of the world, both domestic and wild, and the reindeer, along with Caspian seals and Arctic hare, provide a steady source of food for the wolves.

The Eurasian tundra wolf population is listed as fully viable, although it may only range in 50 to 70 percent of its former territory. In much of the region, wolves are regarded as pests, and there is little movement toward changing that attitude. Oil exploration has increased without any concern for the environment, which could have a devastating effect on the wildlife, including the Eurasian tundra wolf.

Eurasian wolves huddle together to conserve heat but always keep alert for any sign of activity. (Photo © Konrad Wothe/Ellis Nature Photography)

Eurasian Wolf (*Canis lupus lupus*)

The recent merging of several subspecies into the *Canis lupus lupus* category has given this wolf a huge range with diverse habitats, from the steppes of China to the newly reclaimed areas around Brandenburg, Germany, east of Berlin. The Eurasian wolf population is roughly estimated at 100,000 animals, tallied by reports from countries that keep count for research, hunting, trapping, and persecution. The current wide distribution of these wolves is the result of human activities pushing wolves into the more remote regions of Russia, Kazakhstan, and Mongolia. In addition, the wolf is creeping into former strongholds in Western Europe, where they once were savagely perse-cuted as a menace. Vast amounts of strychnine were used to poison wolves. There have also been other problems, such as hybridization with stray feral dogs, attacks by renegade wild dogs, inbreeding depression, and rabies.

It is generally thought that Eurasian wolves fed on human carcasses left by early wars and epidemics such as the plague. But there are no recorded incidents of wolves eating dead bodies during more recent events such as World War I, World War II, or the war in Bosnia. However, there is good evidence that rabid wolves attacked humans on several occasions.

This wolf of Eurasia is almost identical in size and behavior to that of the plains wolf of North America. Standing 30 inches (76 cm) at the shoulder, males weigh approximately 70–130 pounds (32–59 kg); females are 20 percent smaller. The heaviest known Eurasian wolf weighed 158 pounds (71 kg) when it was killed in Romania. There is a wide range in pelt color, with combinations of white, cream, red, gray, and black. The young are born in late April and May with an average of six pups. In their southern range, such as in Spain, the wolves roam in smaller packs of one to three animals and primarily feed on red deer, roe deer, and wild boar. Densities of two wolves per 100 square miles (260 sq. km) are the norm for this region. The pack sizes and territories are larger in the northern regions, where wolves prey on wider-ranging moose and reindeer, thus expanding a wolf's territory to over 1,000 square miles (2600 sq. km) in the far north. Other prey include mufflon (mountain sheep), chamois, hare, saiga antelope, and livestock.

Although wolf numbers recovered slightly during and after major wars when humans faced other prob-lems, Eurasian wolves have suffered dramatically from the consequences of civilization. Overhunting of natural prey and overdevelopment of land have invited wolves into the stockyards, and domestic animals are a significant food source for Eurasian wolves. Reported depredation numbers tend to be higher in countries where there is compensation. But in Kazakhstan, the 60,000 wolves—locally known as "beasts"—supposedly kill 175,000 sheep, goats, cows, and camels annually, without compensation for losses. There are recent reports of wolves allegedly attacking people in the eastern regions of the country, and a bounty for wolves has just been established. Romania reports that 20 percent of the wolves' diet is livestock. Wolf legislation, hunting rules, their status as pests, general attitudes regarding wolves, and depredation compensation are different in each country. This threatens the Eurasian wolf, which understands scent-marked borders. The wolf desperately needs corridors of good habitat with adequate prey in adjoining countries for survival. Fragmented habitat forces wolves to cross into civilized areas, where they may be tempted to eat livestock or be shot. For example, Poland has partial protection with a season to trap wolves, but in the neighboring Czech Republic, there is no legal protection. It is more complicated in Spain where the 2,000 wolves account for more than $1,000,000 in annual livestock damage, yet only certain provinces have compensation policies, so citizens have polarized attitudes about the wolf's existence. It has been found that only 16 percent of the wolves in Spain create most of the problems. Some of these wolves now claim the sunflower fields as territories, consuming hares and livestock under the eyes of Spaniards.

Game warden Tomislav Sporer legally killed one of the last wolves in Croatia before the species gained full protection in 1995. He had killed seventeen wolves in his lifetime, but now he is helping to save the 50 to 100 hundred wolves that live in Croatia. (Photo © Alojzije Frkovic)

In the eastern range of the Russian Federation and China, the wolf has been called a "catastrophe," and most people want complete elimination of this predator. Little money for research, inventory, or education exists. China claims the wolves live in only 20 percent of their former habitat in the northern regions of the country, but wolves are on the increase in Russia, as mentioned earlier, due to the recent changes in government, which caused human economic hardship and left little money for aerial fuel for wolf hunting.

Wolves have benefited from the environmental revolution of the 1970s in some European countries, but nothing has been more dramatic than the changes in war-torn Croatia. Attitudes seemed to shift from persecution to preservation in 1994, which was declared "Year of the Wolf" with a commemorative stamp and posters outlining the need to conserve the 50 to 100 wolves living in the country. Similar wolf education campaigns and research are mounting throughout Europe. Another important component of these projects is the message that wolves must be managed to minimize conflicts with humans.

Indian Wolf (*Canis lupus pallipes*)

Only a handful of studies exist on this small, lightly colored wolf, which ranges in parts of India, Turkey, Iran, and Israel. As with most wolves, their habitat consists of small pockets of land bordering civilization. The Indian wolf is one of the smallest gray wolf subspecies, weighing between 40 and 55 pounds (18–25 kg) and stands 18 to 30 inches (46–76 cm) tall. It closely resembles the red wolf of North America in size and in the shape of the skull.

This wolf lives in arid and semi-arid grasslands, rarely stepping into the forests. In the northern steppe regions, the Indian wolf tends to be bigger and have larger packs and territories than in the southern arid areas. The physical size difference suggests the northern wolves may have bred with a larger subspecies. Each of the countries in this wolf's range commonly call *C. l. pallipes* after the name of their nation; for example, the Indian wolf is the same subspecies as the Israeli wolf.

The wolf is listed as endangered in India. Despite this classification, it has received limited conservation efforts, and legal action after wolf killings is difficult. About 1,500 wolves are thought to live in the desert and shrub land areas of the western Indian peninsula, in nature parks, and in the large wild areas set aside as religious shrines. A study in Velavadar National Park in western India found that wolves preying on natural prey such as blackbuck, a species of dwarf antelope native to India, formed packs of six to fourteen members, whereas wolves relying on domestic livestock had smaller packs of one to four wolves.

Indian wolves give birth to an average litter of six in December or January. A wolf often returns to the same denning site each year, which consists of dug-up fox holes, dry riverbeds, embankments, or even drainage pipes. The pups are moved to three or four rendezvous sites before they begin to travel with the entire pack at around six months of age.

In India, snatching children, or "lifting" as it is called locally, by wolves is a common allegation, and it is often rumored that people who have suddenly disappeared have been killed by wolves. But documentation of such incidents is scarce. However, such thinking, as well as wolf predation on livestock, impedes the conservation process. The fact that wolves still exist in this crowded country is probably due to religious tolerance of all living creatures and the scarcity of firearms.

Israel has protected its small population of 200 to 300 wolves since 1954, but the country did not enforce the law until ten years later, when the wolf was almost extinct due to mass strychnine poisoning. The Israeli wolf primarily lives in the rift valley and the southern Negev Desert, but it is thought that about fifty wolves live in the Golan Heights. As in India, the wolves are smaller in the southern region and gradually increase in size in the north.

The northern wolves also tend to have darker coats.

From 1914 to 1948, the wolves in the region were nearly eradicated by an anti-rabies campaign and by angry cattle breeders. Today, collisions with automobiles are the main mortality factor. In addition, wolf-dog hybrids may roam the country, adding to the conflicts with humans. The wild prey of wolves in this region includes gazelles, hares, rodents, wild pigs, and ibex, but wolves are also seen raiding garbage and sometimes preying on livestock. But they are well protected by Israel's law, and the attitude of the public is changing. The recent peace talks with Syria over the Golan Heights has concerned many wolf experts, because Syria and most other Middle East countries persecute wolves.

The wolves of the Middle East and India are in jeopardy due to the lack of natural habitat and limited water supplies that are reserved for livestock. (Photo © Roni Sofer)

Interestingly, some Israeli wolf researchers think the female wolves rear their pups without help from the male. In addition, several reports indicate that this smaller wolf subspecies seldom howls, which may be a behavioral adaptation that makes it more difficult for humans to locate wolves, or perhaps there are so few wolves that territories are not well established. Then again, it may be just another wolf mystery.

Arabian Wolf (*Canis lupus arabs*)

The Arabian wolf is the smallest and possibly the least-known wolf subspecies. It weighs approximately 40 pounds (18 kg) and stands 26 inches (66 cm) at the shoulders. The wolf's pale-colored pelage helps camouflage it in its desert habitat. This wolf has only a thin coat since it roams among the Arabian sand dunes, one of the most arid areas in the world. Its ears are quite large in comparison with northern wolves, which not only aids in hearing but allows heat to escape, keeping the wolf slightly cooler.

The Arabian wolf ranges throughout the Arabian peninsula, and recently some wolves were seen in protected areas near the Jordanian-Iraqi border. Some experts believe the wolf in southern Israel is actually *Canis lupus arabs*.

Short, thin fur covers the small Arabian wolf, making its appearance look pale and delicate in comparison to its northern cousins. This wolf lives on the edge of the great Arabian sand dunes, one of the world's most arid regions. (Photo © Roni Sofer)

Local and international experts conducted the first survey of Arabian wolves in late 1991. The researchers visited several areas where tracks were seen and wolves were heard howling. Ironically, many of the wolf reports came from angry shepherds, who still hang dead wolf carcasses from trees or posts as revenge against this predator, which they claim kills many of their animals. Preliminary research indicated that the wolf population seems to be widespread and stable, with a population of 600 to 700 wolves.

Some of the best information on Arabian wolves comes from the few that exist in captivity. Their smaller weight has been documented, and breeding activity occurs in January and February, with the birth of five or six pups two months later. These desert wolves seem to lack the bond of a pack and are often seen hunting alone or in pairs.

Desert conditions force wild and domestic animals to live near the limited water sources, which provides the wolves with equal opportunities to feed on livestock, as well as wild hares, rodents, and ungulates. Arabian wolves also forage through rubbish and eat road-killed animals and dead livestock. During the intense heat, the wolves will dig deep into the sand seeking cooler temperatures. They are primarily a nocturnal hunter, except during the cooler winter months when they are often seen during the day.

The future of the Arabian wolf is still in question. The farmers and shepherds are resentful of the presence of wolves and shoot or poison them whenever possible. Depredation statistics are few, and no legislation has been introduced for compensation to farmers and shepherds. Efforts are underway by the National Commission for Wildlife Conservation and Development of Saudi Arabia to officially include the wolf on the threatened species list, which would be followed by a wolf management plan to ensure the survival of the Arabian wolf.

Wolf-Dog Hybrid (*Canis lupus?*)

Combining the wildness of a wolf with the trainability of a domestic dog has created a new animal—and launched a new controversy. It is called a wolf-dog hybrid. These hybrids lack a scientific name in general until the specific wolf and domestic breeds are identified, and then it is still unclear. Most often wolves are bred with German shepherds, malamutes, or huskies, breeds which maintain the large size, long fur, and coloring of the wild wolf. However, it is possible to breed wolves with any type of dog.

The content of pure wolf blood often raises the monetary value of the animal, but the percentage usually lacks both genetic and biological science. Although a pure wolf and a pure dog will produce a 50/50 hybrid, it is difficult to assess which genes are passed to the next generation when these animals are bred with other hybrids.

A trained eye may distinguish a hybrid from a wild wolf by noticing the taller ears, longer snout, and a winter coat that lacks the furry jaw tufts of a wolf. The sexual maturity rate is unpredictable with hybrids. Female wolves reach sexual maturity at two to four years of age and have one estrus cycle per year. Domestic female dogs reach sexual maturity at around eight months of age and have two estrus cycles per year. Domestic male dogs mature close to eight months of age when they usually begin to demonstrate raised-leg urination. Male wolves do not mature until two or three years of age. The hybrid maturity rate usually varies somewhere in between.

The life span of a hybrid can reach twelve to fourteen years of age, or equal to that of a wolf in captivity or a large dog. However, the average life span is usually only three years, because of the aggression of mature hybrids and the typical owner's failure to address this behavior through proper training. This aggressive nature can result in a bite or an attack, and the owner is usually faced with destroying the animal.

The compatibility of a wolf and a dog as a hybrid is questionable. Wolves cannot be housebroken or well trained, whereas dogs are capable of both. Eager owners forget that domestication takes many years of selective breeding and that a few generations will not eliminate predatory instincts. To a wolf-dog hybrid, a small child running or screaming can look like distressed prey. The wolf predatory instincts can take over without warning, and this sometimes can be fatal. Each year, there are numerous attacks by hybrids on people and several deaths, primarily of

Wolf-dog hybrids share characteristics of both subspecies, which makes them unpredictable. This hybrid was reputedly seven-eighths wolf. (Photo © Lynn and Donna Rogers)

children. Wild wolves are naturally frightened of humans, but wolf-dog hybrids are imprinted on people and show no fear. By 1991 in the United States, the wolf-dog hybrid replaced the pit bull as the macho canine of choice. The hybrid has special appeal in the U.S., which has approximately 300,000 to 1,000,000 of these animals. The estimates are so varied because many owners hide the fact that they own hybrids due to laws that are quickly banning them from cities. Their numbers are relatively low in Europe, and many wolf experts are trying to prevent any wolf-dog hybrid problems from arising through education about their danger and new legislation.

Experts say hybrids should be properly hand-raised together, at least as a pair, and live in a high, double-fenced, locked enclosure. A minimum of two professionally trained people need to make a life commitment to the animals and learn about wolf behavior and proper instruction to ensure the hybrids are never treated as dogs. Proper permits must be maintained, and neighbors should be consulted before the purchase of a hybrid as a pet. Small children under fourteen should not be allowed near the animals, and special veterinary care and a meat diet are essential.

Few people are willing to take responsibility for the expense and time needed for properly raising a wolf-dog hybrid. The consequent tragedies often affect the image of the wild wolf. When wolf-dog hybrids attack children, it is the wolf part of the animal that gets the negative media attention.

Domestic Dog (*Canis lupus familiaris*)

That favorite human companion that retrieves your slippers and protects your home is more wild than you may think. In 1993, the domestic dog was proclaimed the same species as the wolf by the *Mammal Species of the World: A Taxonomic and Geographic Reference*, the final authority of the scientific community on mammal classification. Pet dogs were originally thought to be a separate species, *Canis familiaris*. This new classification is debated, however, especially in reference to the difference in skulls. The classic definition of a species is a group of organisms capable of reproducing among one another. Wolves, coyotes, and domestic dogs can all interbreed, although it is rare under natural conditions.

It has long been thought that domestic dogs evolved from wolves, and recent molecular genetic analysis seems to confirm this theory. The wolf was the first wild animal to be domesticated, and some records indicate this initially occurred in Central Europe approximately 15,000 years ago. People tamed young wolf pups by nursing them with human milk. Over time, they were used as hunting companions, to guard settlements, and to help women with child care by cleaning fecal material from the babies. This child care technique is still used by some tribal women in Africa.

The companionship of humans and dogs had major historical implications. It increased the success of hunting expeditions, because dogs could track and corner animals injured by arrows. The success of hunting drastically reduced prey species, which forced humans to migrate and spread out to new continents over the next

5,000 years. Then some cultures in the Middle East learned to grow wild grains and to domesticate wild sheep and goats. Dogs were bred for herding livestock and, ironically, for protecting domestic animals from their wild ancestors.

Today, selective breeding of domestic dogs for hunting, herding, protection, and companionship has spread to 138 breeds, as recognized by the American Kennel Club. Additional breeds are found in canine clubs around the world, which also register and compete in confirmation show rings. The smallest dog is the Chihuahua that must weigh under 6 pounds (2.7 kg) to be official, while the largest is the mastiff, weighing 175 to 190 pounds (79–86 kg). The male Irish wolfhound is the tallest at 32 inches (81 cm).

These breeds are quite a stretch from the image of the wild wolf, but their behavior is strikingly similar. Male dogs will scent-mark their territory, and the urine of another dog will stimulate a male to mark or urinate over it to establish its territory. Dogs have an inherited good sense of smell; they will bury their nose into the ground to interpret a variety of signs left by other dogs. Scratching the ground also spreads their mark by releasing special scent chemicals from between their toes. Loud sirens or other high-pitched sounds will excite dogs, and they may bark, yelp, or howl in return. All of these behaviors are common to the wild wolf.

Labrador retrievers make excellent pets, displaying the strong bonding and loyal characteristics evident in wild wolves. These dogs formed a pack with their owner, Code Sternal. (Photo © Nancy Gibson)

Perhaps most interestingly, dogs bond with their owners, similar to relationships between members of a wolf pack. It is this loyalty and emotional attachment that endear us to dogs. Ironically, humans have historically misunderstood and even hated the wolf. Meanwhile, wolflike behaviors are the principal component of our daily, intimate relationship with "our best friend."

The territorial howl of a wolf often led humans to their hiding places. Experienced hunters learned to howl to entice wolves to return their call and thus reveal their location for trapping and poisoning. (Photo © Scot Stewart)

War on Wolves

Wild, furry animals with big teeth have always been a source of emotional conflict for humans. While many large predators produce a sense of wariness, no animal is more misunderstood and has sparked more controversy than the wolf. It is the only animal on which humans declared war. Yet the wolf survived some of the most intensive and prolonged extermination practices in history, and these campaigns were based on fiction not fact.

The transition of the wolf's image from founder of the domestic dog to villainous foe had more to do with human behavior than that of wolves. To achieve "civilization," the wilderness had to be tamed, and each generation became less acquainted with the natural behavior of wildlife. The domestication of cows, sheep, and goats produced the career of farming, and the wolf became the top competitor to people raising animals. Feasting on a wild deer or domestic cow had equal value on the menu. Hence, domestication of animals triggered a feud that still rankles the minds of many people and captures newspaper headlines around the world.

Though wolves were likely persecuted all the way back to the beginnings of domestication, evidence of the war against the wolf first appeared in Christian carvings around 900 A.D., such as those depicting Christ on the cross above the wolf in "Rambona Diptych." The carvings depict a triumphant Christ on a cross with the Latin inscription "I am Jesus of Nazareth, King of Jews." Below the cross is a large wolf with the pagans Romulus and Remus and another Latin inscription stating, "Romulus and Remus fed by the wolf." This justaposition symbolizes the victory of Christ over the religion of pagan Rome, whose barbarism seems to be reflected in the savage expression of the wolf.

The wolf killings spread throughout much of western Europe in a fierce fight to conquer this legendary creature that was thought to be a bloodthirsty killing machine. Their bad reputation may have been nurtured during the Black Plague in the Middle Ages, when so-called ravenous wolves stalked the countryside eating the dead human carcasses. It is difficult to find the truth in the early battle against wolves, since much of the information is interwoven in folklore. Yet there is no doubt that the negative attitude about wolves was widespread.

People killed wolves at every opportunity with every conceivable method. Primitive tools, such as pikes and spearlike instruments, were used to batter wolf pups and their parents. Villagers would form huge circles in the countryside, then move inward making loud noises and beating the ground with sticks to force the wolves into a small area. The villagers would then kill them. More people, tools, and guns only meant more harm to the European wolf population, which was either eliminated or shoved into small, remnant pockets of land inaccessible to humans. Wolves were exterminated in England by 1486. In Scotland, the last wolf was killed in 1743, and the Irish celebrated the "defeat of the wild" with the death of the last wolf in 1776. France lost its last wolf in the 1920s, although a few returned to the French Alps in 1992.

Eastern Europe never completely lost their wolves. But the population is presently quite low, and many wolves are still hunted with the intensity of earlier centuries. The fact that there are any wolves left in Europe is usually credited to the widespread use of strychnine, an inexpensive poison that was readily available to people. Experienced wolves soon learned to detect strychnine. The wolves would eat small amounts of the laced food, taste the poison, and then avoid the rest of the meal. Limited amounts of the poison would make the wolves sick, but they survived. In addition, wolves became wise to some types of traps and avoided humans at all costs.

After the passage of the Endangered Species Act in 1973, which gave wolves full protection, some wolves were snared illegally by angry farmers. Farmers commonly referred to the killings as the "three Ss"—shoot (or snare), shovel, and shut-up. (Photo © Lynn and Donna Rogers)

In Japan, the positive image of the wolf was etched into the Shinto shrines, in part because Buddhist doctrine revered wolves. People would pray for wolves to come to their land and kill the animals that were eating their crops. The feudal powers between the sixteenth and nineteenth centuries prohibited the average citizen from hunting game, and wildlife maintained some balance. But in 1868, a new government allowed hunting, and the wolf population plummeted, ending in the extermination of the species around 1910. A variety of traps, poisons, and firearms, fueled by negative attitudes, led to the wolf's demise in Japan.

The Europeans, of course, traveled to North America, and they carried along their hatred of the wolf and the self-anointed duty to destroy it. Samuel Williams, an early Vermont historian, wrote in his book, *Native Animals,* "One of the most common and noxious of all our animals is the wolf….This animal is extremely fierce, sanguinous and carnivorous. When a number of them associate it is not for peace but for war and destruction." The first wolf bounty was established on November 9, 1630, in Boston, Massachusetts, just a decade after the Pilgrims landed in the New World. In 1756, John Adams wrote about the arrival of the colonists in America: "the whole continent was one continued dismal wilderness, the haunt of wolves and bears and more savage men."

A wolf tracks through the Minnesota wilderness, where the national campaign to wipe out this species failed. Four hundred to six hundred wolves survived the ordeal. (Photo © Lynn and Donna Rogers)

Thus, a well-documented wolf war began in North America, with fanatical righteousness. The United States government paid generous bounties for dead wolves, making it a profitable and rewarding business. Fifty-five thousand wolves were killed each year between 1870 and 1877. But enough wolves remained in 1914 for the federal government to launch a campaign to rid U.S. lands of the remaining wolves and other predators once and for all. The U.S. government provided poison and personnel, unlike other parts of the world. President Theodore Roosevelt, a noted naturalist, described the wolf as a "beast of waste and desolation."

.F. ERBEN, GRAZ.

An Austrian hunter shows off his kill of a six-year-old wolf in the southern Carinthia region. A monument at the site reads, "Farmers' Nightmare Ended on March 4, 1914 by the Gräflich-Henchelschen hunter, Paul Steinbauer."

Unprecedented vengeance accompanied the war on wolves in the U.S., with most people thinking they were protecting livestock, as well as deer, caribou, and moose. The government hired former buffalo hunters, who had successfully wiped out that species and were looking for a new job of destruction. Beginning as early as 1860, "wolfers," as they were called, were equipped with large amounts of strychnine poison, which was placed on dead carcasses. Such violent means spread like a wave across the western prairies, deserts, mountains, and even the national parks, which were supposedly set aside to be wild. The poison intended for wolves was indiscriminate, so foxes, coyotes, bears, mountain lions, and other predators died also. Unlike Europeans, Americans began to use an effective tasteless poison called compound 1080, or sodium fluoroacetate. The poison was distributed to more than a thousand bait stations in the U.S. and southern Canada in 1956, and the wolf shortly thereafter took its last breath in most of America.

Other techniques included live trapping wolves and then infecting them with mange, a highly contagious skin disease that would wipe out a pack when the wolf was later released. Wolf dens were dug up, and the excavated pups were strangled, shot, or sometimes collected to show the public during their cute puppy age, only to be later destroyed. Traps were set in every known wolf location, and hounds were used to help locate wolf packs and dens.

Some western ranchers still tell tales of capturing live wolves, tying ropes around each leg, and then simultaneously pulling each leg off while the ranchers celebrated and watched the wolf's slow, painful death. Even

Wolf tracks are now a common sight along northern Minnesota logging roads and trails. The clear-cut forest attracts whitetailed deer, the main diet for these wolves. (Photo © Lynn and Donna Rogers)

some western roads were supposedly paved with dead wolf carcasses.

The savage war against the wolf was a success, and by 1926 wolves were wiped out in most areas, including Yellowstone National Park, and wolf populations were extremely fragmented where they did survive. Minnesota was the only contiguous state where the anti-wolf campaign had failed; a small population of 400 to 600 wolves survived in the northern forests. The last bounty for a wolf killed in Minnesota ($35) was paid in 1967. In 1973, the gray wolf was listed as an endangered species in the U.S., and the federal government then had to reverse its position and address a recovery plan for the wolf.

In Minnesota, what was once considered a failure to exterminate wolves later turned out to be a success. Attitudes toward the wolf started to change, initiated by research and new information on the state's wolves. Earth Day, and other environmental events, questioned the ecological imbalance of large ungulate herds without natural predators overgrazing vast areas, spreading disease, and colliding with automobiles. Wolves ignored the international borders and traveled south from Ontario into Minnesota, filling every suitable area for wolves in the state. They then spread east to Wisconsin and Michigan, as well as west to North and South Dakota.

In the last twenty-five years, the wolf has gained a new status, championed as the symbol of the lost wilderness and the natural solution to overpopulation of ungulates. Wolf lovers began to shout at government officials as loud as the wolf haters. The government traded the wolf bounties for compensation checks to farmers who lost livestock to wolves. In addition, the government has sponsored and acted on wolf recovery plans for the red wolf in the southeastern U.S. and for the gray wolf in Yellowstone National Park and central Idaho. Mexican wolf recovery plans are in process.

Despite this good news for the wolf, the war against this species most likely will continue, as people are bitterly divided on the issue. The fortunes of wolves are hard to separate from the politics of humans that create dramatic contradictions about wolves. Eradication and recovery of wolves has been expensive, and the burden of their future lies in the dispersal of solid biological information to the right people in order to exercise compromise—not another war.

The statuesque appearance of a black wolf certainly appeals to wildlife advocates worldwide, though black wolves are most commonly found in Canada. (Photo © Lynn and Donna Rogers)

Wolves can travel long distances in search of food and security. This high mobility is an asset for wolves but a challenge for researchers who want to follow and study them. (Photo © Scot Stewart)

Recovery and Reintroduction

If wolves are to survive they must have food and security. For either of these requirements to be sustained, some adjustments in human attitudes are necessary. Wolves prefer wild food, but they will eat livestock. This preying on livestock, as well as the loss of suitable habitat, has seriously hampered their security. Biologically, wolves are a resilient species. They have a high reproduction rate, with an average of six pups a year, and high mobility, dispersing long distances from their natal pack. A healthy source population of wolves can usually overcome heavy hunting and trapping in a surrounding area. The key is to maintain the source population.

Human tolerance of wolves has many barriers, but knowledge gained from scientific studies has moderated the wolf's reputation as a villain. Farmers and ranchers who have always lived with wolves face the realities of living with a predator, and most argue for quick compensation for loss of livestock rather than extermination of wolves. Whereas other livestock owners prefer to keep the predators away, using anecdotal stories and legends to prove their point. In a 1995 judicial hearing about the wolf reintroduction in Yellowstone National Park and Idaho, a farmer told the judge that he had "a farmer friend in Minnesota where the wolves ate all the deer, all the cows and now they were eating all the dogs." In truth, wolves eat less than one percent of the livestock living in Minnesota's wolf range. Wolf advocates also use anecdotes to save the wolf, and in some instances, they have even placed the importance of a wolf's life higher than that of a human's.

The Endangered Species Act of 1973 gave the wolf full protection in the continental United States and formed recovery teams for the red and gray wolf. At the time, wolves only lived in the wildernesses of Minnesota and Alaska.

Minnesota and neighboring Ontario had the key source population of wolves. That element, teamed with improved public attitudes, new laws, and favorable publicity, has allowed the wolves of this region to quickly recover in Minnesota and bordering states—and to live in areas not intended in the recovery plans. A wolf was recently radio-tracked within eighteen miles (29 km) of Saint Paul, Minnesota, well south of its primary range, demonstrating that wolves are more adaptable than originally thought.

In other areas of the country, wolf projects needed intense help from humans, as the source popu-

Romanian researchers in the Carpathian Mountains track wolves using telemetry and snowmobiles. In addition to such scientific work, wolf ecotourism is a budding business in Romania. (Photo © Christoph Promberger, Munich Wildlife Society)

lation did not exist. Sometimes such efforts sparked controversy. The red wolf reintroduction in the southeastern U.S. in the early 1990s caused little stir, but the 1995 reintroduction of wolves to Yellowstone National Park and Idaho was preceded by extensive debate. In 1944, renowned author and conservationist, Aldo Leopold, suggested that wolves should live in Yellowstone and the adjacent preserves. The long process did not begin until 1974, when biologists entered into the political and public arenas with the known facts on wolves. Wolf advocates and haters battled their cause through the media and Congress while the whole world watched. In 1991, Congress directed the U.S. Fish and Wildlife Service to draft an Environmental Impact Statement (EIS) on the reintroduction of wolves to the region. It was the most extensive public process ever conducted concerning a natural resource, including 130 public hearings across the nation. The public spoke and wrote with a vengeance; 170,000 comments were received. This was the largest response in history for a proposed federal action, and the vast majority wanted wolves back in Yellowstone and Idaho.

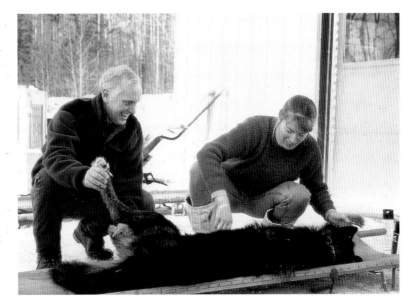

Walter Medwid, director of the International Wolf Center, and Dr. Janet Jones apply a lice preventative to one of the Yellowstone wolves, the final examination procedure for each of the sixty-six wolves that were shipped to the park and Idaho in 1995 and 1996. (Photo © Nancy Gibson)

Ranchers and environmental groups fought each other every step of the way, and lawsuits are still pending, despite the initial twenty-nine wolves that were brought from Canada to Idaho and Yellowstone National Park in January 1995. In Idaho, the fifteen wolves were "hard released," set free immediately upon arrival. The fourteen Yellowstone wolves were collected as packs and kept in acclimation pens for ten weeks.

Animal Damage Control officers shot one wolf on February 6, 1996, after it was determined the wolf killed livestock. Two wolves have been shot illegally. A landowner shot one shortly after the wolf was released in Idaho. The man claimed the wolf killed a young calf, but the calf was later determined to have been stillborn. The second wolf was shot as it roamed north of the Yellowstone Park border. A generous reward helped to reveal the offender, who had beheaded the wolf, skinned it, and kept it in his home. He was later found guilty and served six months in jail for killing the large, 122-pound (55 kg) wolf tagged R10, the only single male brought to Yellowstone. Researchers had paired him with a female and her nine-month-old pup. They successfully bred, and the female gave birth to eight pups while she waited his return. The mother and pups had to be collected and brought back to captivity to ensure their survival. Four and a half months later, the mother and pups were set free, and a new male mate from one of the other Yellowstone packs was waiting to assume the alpha duties. Tragically, one of the male pups was hit by a truck in December 1995, But the surviving pack members are doing well. Biologists were pleasantly surprised by the birth of the eight pups; another pack produced at least one pup. In

Four one-acre (0.4 hectare) acclimation pens were built for the wolf packs reintroduced in Yellowstone National Park. (Photo © L. David Mech)

addition, seventeen more wolves were placed in Yellowstone and twenty in Idaho in 1996. The goal of ten breeding pairs or 100 wolves will complete the recovery project.

It is generally thought that Mexican wolf recovery will benefit from the success of the Yellowstone and Idaho projects. As mentioned earlier, biologists are breeding captive Mexican wolves in several centers in the U.S. and Mexico. Two sites in the wolf's historic range have been chosen for possible release, and the Environmental Impact Statement for this project is in its final draft. The plan calls for establishing a self-sustaining population of at least 100 Mexican wolves in their former mid- to high-elevation range in the southwestern U.S.

A captive Mexican wolf peers out from the edge of its enclosure. The decision to reintroduce Mexican wolves may depend on human reactions to the wolves in Yellowstone National Park and Idaho. (Photo © Tom and Pat Leeson)

Other parts of the world are also initiating studies of wolf recovery. Voluntary efforts are underway in Scotland to replace the wolves that were killed off in the seventeenth century. The Scottish Highlands is a vast region with low human density and a burgeoning population of 300,000 red deer and almost 100,000 roe deer. Some experts claim that a wolf population of 150 to 200 animals could easily survive in the 15,500 square mile (40,300 sq. km) area. But farmers and shepherds, who have more than one million sheep in the same area, oppose the wolf's return. The government has been reluctant to address the wolf recovery issue, despite a 1992 directive from the European Union and a recommendation from the Berne Convention in 1979, which promoted the protection of wolves. An environmental impact study may persuade the government, but a non-profit group will need to fund it in cooperation with government officials, as there are no forthcoming public funds to finance it.

The idea of wolves returning to Scotland has caused quite a lot of excitement. In a BBC television poll, 75 percent of the respondents favored wolf reintroduction. The message of wolf advocates, who justify the need for wolves in order to balance the ungulate populations and stimulate ecotourism, seems to be the dominant line of thinking.

Plans to reintroduce wolves in Japan is a surprise to some people, including the Japanese themselves. The Japanese ranching community is new, relatively small, and poses few obstacles to the return of the wolf. The major problem facing wolf recovery is little public concern for the species. Two wolf subspecies, *Canis lupus hattai* and *Canis lupus hodophilax*, became extinct in Japan around 1900, and the populations of wild boar, sika deer, and serow have expanded to such a degree that natural forests cannot regenerate, which leads to soil erosion. Hunting of deer has also decreased, exacerbating the problem. Preliminary efforts are underway to reintroduce wolves on the northern island of Hokkaido. The first step was a survey sent to one thousand people, but only 6 percent responded favorably to the wolf's return. The overwhelming response was that wolves are harmful to humans, and there is little suitable land left for large carnivores, though neither of these beliefs are true. Both issues need to be addressed, so educating the public has become the next challenge. The media has shown a strong interest, and a large wolf conference in Japan in 1996 will assemble world experts and add muscle to the plight of the wolves in Japan. If successful, China would be the likely source of the reintroduced wolves.

Two pups huddle near their den in Montana. Wolves have naturally recolonized northwestern Montana since 1986. Approximately seventy-five wolves moved down from Canada. (Photo © Alan and Sandy Carey)

Reintroduction efforts are extremely costly, time consuming, labor intensive, and divisive. Wolves that have recolonized former habitat in Europe have proven to be less expensive—but every bit as controversial. Italy's stable population of wolves has crossed the mountains and crept back into old strongholds in Mercantour National Park in the French Alps, but each step of those wolves has been scrutinized by the public. Many national parks in France and Europe are used by shepherds, and they resent the wolves eating their sheep. Renegade wild dogs may be causing some of the problems, but wolves are most often blamed. However, the French government helps finance prevention measures for the shepherds, and a non-profit group provides some compensation.

Poland's wolves have expanded west into Germany with mixed reviews, and Slovakia and Romania are conducting new wolf studies. Switzerland is preparing for natural wolf migration, such as what happened in neighboring France. But hatred of wolves in Europe is as deeply ingrained as are the historic buildings and narrow streets. Wolf restoration in most countries will have to overcome the "big bad wolf" attitude of many Europeans.

Most experts agree that European wolves will have to be controlled in some areas and left alone in others. Compensation for livestock loss will either have to come from the government or non-profit groups, similar to what is being done in the western United States and France. These funds help quell the fears of farmers and shepherds and help minimize animosity toward wolves.

In some parts of the world, the wolf has become a predator that pays. Ecotourism is a fast-growing industry in northern Minnesota, Yellowstone Park, Italy, and now Romania. People want to confront the animal of legends and learn more about it. Wolf art, crafts, T-shirts, books, and jewelry also add new economic value to this predator. But more importantly, wolves and their habitat not only have intrinsic and commercial worth, they also enrich us in ways we cannot measure.

Recovery of wolves has been a slow and difficult road to travel. Wolf management comes with a price tag, and it is our burden to get the right information to the right people, so they can make the right decisions. From what I have experienced, this is not easy, and even compromise has left some scars. Due to its public image and predatory behavior, the wolf is the most challenging animal to restore. Thus the Yellowstone National Park and Idaho reintroduction, as well as the red wolf reintroduction in the southeast, were a historic success for wolves—and humans.

Index

Wolf Distribution Maps

These maps reflect what is known about red wolf (*Canis rufus*) and gray wolf (*Canis lupus*) distribution around the world. In many parts of Eurasia, our knowledge of wolves lacks solid biological data, and in some cases, it is gathered by the people who persecute wolves.

Maps by Tricia Hull

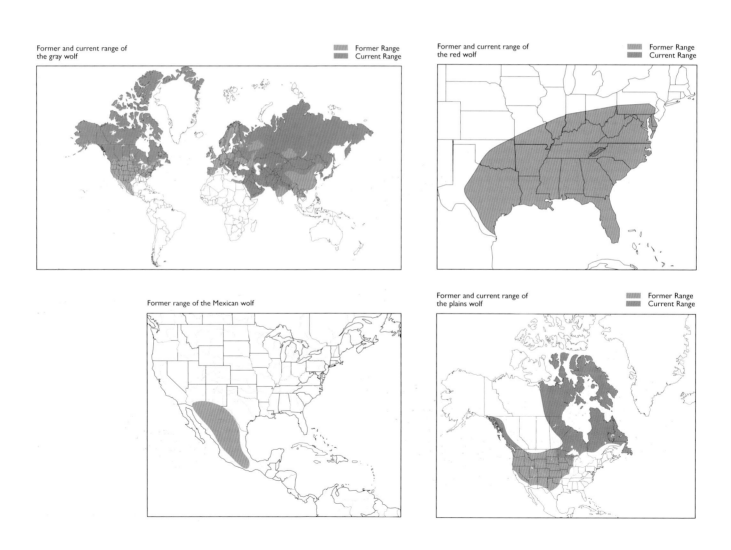

Former and current range of the gray wolf — Former Range, Current Range

Former and current range of the red wolf — Former Range, Current Range

Former range of the Mexican wolf

Former and current range of the plains wolf — Former Range, Current Range

Former and current range of the Arctic wolf

Former and current range of
the Russian tundra wolf

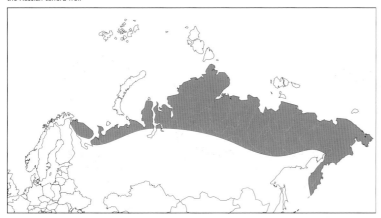

Former range and known viable
populations of the Indian wolf

Former Range
Known populations

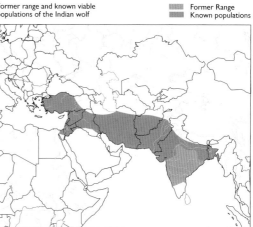

Former and current range of
the Eurasian wolf

Former Range
Current Range

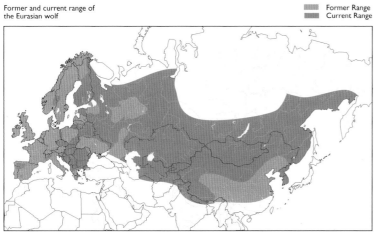

Former range and known viable
populations of the Arabian wolf

Former Range
Known populations

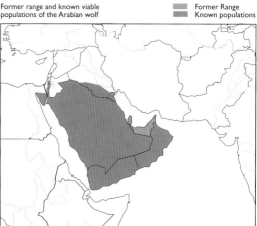

Wolf Facts

2 of 9 species of the genus *Canis*

Family: Canidae

Distributions: North America, Europe, Asia above 20 degrees latitude

1. Gray Wolf- *Canis lupus*

14 wild subspecies: *arctos, occidentalis, nubilus, baileyi,* and *lycaon* in North America. *Albus, communis, lupus, cubanensis, pallipes, arabs, hattai, hodophilax,* and *lupaster* in Eurasia. Domestic: *Canis lupus familiaris*

Names:

English, gray wolf

Spanish, lobo

French, loup

German, Wolf

Description: The largest wild canid. Fur is thick and usually gray, but it can also be black, white, red, or brown.

Weight: 40–140 pounds (18–63 kg)

Height at shoulders: 22–32 inches (56–81 cm)

Head and body length: 40–60 inches (102–152 cm)

Reproduction: Mating occurs January through April. Gestation lasts 61–63 days.

Litter size averages six pups. Age at sexual maturity 22 to 46 months. Longevity is approximately twelve years in the wild.

2. Red Wolf- *Canis rufus*

Description: Slightly smaller wolf with cinnamon- or tawny-colored fur.

Weight: 50–70 pounds (23–32 kg)

Height at shoulders: 20–32 inches (51–81 cm)

Reproduction: Similar to *Canis lupus* except averages five pups per year.

Recommended Reading

The Way of the Wolf by Dr. L. David Mech is an excellent glimpse into the behavior of wolves through the eyes of the world's leading researcher.

The Wolf by Dr. L. David Mech is a classic book for people who want to study the wolf more seriously.

The Wolves of Isle Royale by Rolf O. Peterson describes his twenty-five years of experience on this island, known to many as an ecological lab, studying the ebb and flow of the moose and wolf population.

A Society of Wolves: National Parks and the Battle Over the Wolf, by Rick McIntyre depicts the struggles between wolves and humans, using historical photographs, excellent writing, and interviews. A revised edition, including information about the Yellowstone reintroductions, was recently published.

The Wolves of Yellowstone by Michael K. Phillips and Douglas W. Smith, with photographs by Barry and Teri O'Neill, details the story of the Yellowstone releases of 1995 and 1996. Written by the leaders of the reintroduction project, this is *the* reference work on the historic return of wolves to the park.

The INTERNATIONAL WOLF CENTER is a highly recommended wolf organization based in Minnesota. The Center is dedicated to public education about wolves worldwide. They publish a first-class magazine and numerous educational materials, sponsor symposiums and speakers' bureaus, and have a 17,000-square-foot (5,700-sq.-m) building that houses the award-winning "Wolves and Humans" exhibit, a theater, and four live wolves. The Center also hosts a variety of classes, field studies, and howling adventures in the heart of wolf country. Their address is 1396 Highway 169, Ely, Minnesota, 55731, USA; or call 1-800-ELY-WOLF. You can also e-mail the IWC at wolfinfo@wolf.org or connect to their home page on the internet, http://www.wolf.org.

About the Author

(Photo © Lynn and Donna Rogers)

Nancy Gibson is the naturalist for the Emmy-award-winning PBS show *Newton's Apple*, which is in its fourteenth season. She is also a co-founder of the International Wolf Center and a consultant for the Minnesota Department of Natural Resources, local media, and numerous wildlife-related organizations. She serves on the board of the Bell Museum of Natural History at the University of Minnesota and chairs the Citizen's Advisory Committee of the Environmental Trust Fund. A close associate of Dr. L. David Mech, Nancy travels extensively in the U.S. and abroad to work on and speak about wolf issues. She spent the summers of 1992 and 1993 with Dr. Mech in the High Arctic, producing programming for *Newton's Apple* about the Arctic wolves of the northern tundra. She writes extensively for *International Wolf* magazine and has been a national guest columnist for King Syndicated Services. Nancy, her husband Ron Sternal, and their son Code make their home in Minneapolis, Minnesota.